THE OFFICIAL
Liverpool FC
ANNUAL 2011

Written by Paul Eaton

Designed by Alice Lake-Hammond

A Grange Publication

© 2010. Published by Grange Communications Ltd., Edinburgh under licence from The Liverpool Football Club and Athletic Grounds Ltd. Printed in the EU.

ISBN: 978-1-907104-67-1

£7.99

CONTENTS

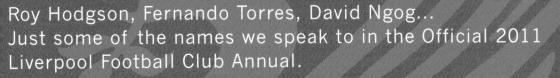

INTRODUCTION

Roy Hodgson, Fernando Torres, David Ngog...
Just some of the names we speak to in the Official 2011
Liverpool Football Club Annual.

There are extensive interviews with recent major signings
Joe Cole and Milan Jovanovic. We also talk to England
youth internationals Jonjo Shelvey and Martin Kelly,
Argentina winger Maxi Rodriguez and Brazilian
midfielder Lucas Leiva – LFC Young Player of
the Year for Season 2009/10.

The Annual also spotlights the
contribution of Liverpool FC
players at the World Cup
in South Africa as well as
looking at the Club's new
medical set-up through the
eyes of Peter Brukner, new
Head of Sports Medicine
and Sports Science.

We look back at the last
year at LFC and look
forward to a bright future
under a new manager.

SEASON REVIEW

AUGUST

Liverpool FC kicked off the season full of hope and optimism, but fell to an opening day defeat at Tottenham before a 4-0 drubbing of Stoke restored some confidence to the Anfield ranks. Unfortunately, a home defeat to Aston Villa followed on a Monday night at Anfield before a mixed opening month finished with a thrilling 3-2 victory at Bolton.

SEPTEMBER

The Reds hit newly-promoted Burnley for four as they kicked off a new month in style, and a 1-0 victory over Debrecen in their opening Champions League fixture of the campaign sent out positive signs for the future. Carling Cup progress was secured with a narrow victory over Leeds, while Hull felt the full force of a rampant Reds as they were hit for six at Anfield. Disappointment followed, however, as Fiorentina inflicted European defeat on Rafael Benitez's men in Italy.

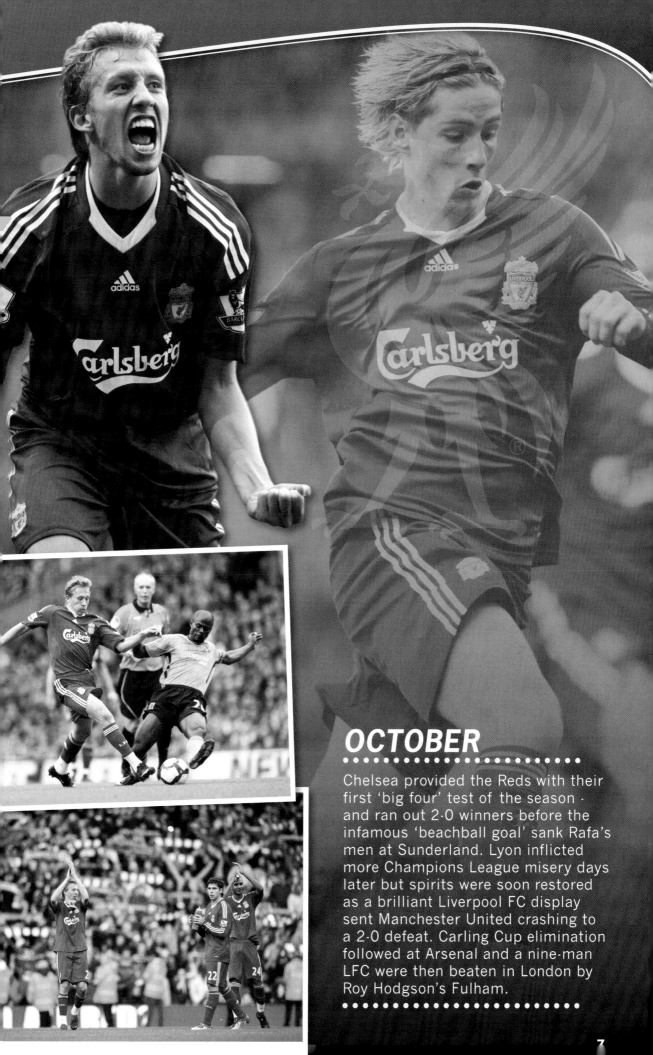

OCTOBER

Chelsea provided the Reds with their first 'big four' test of the season - and ran out 2-0 winners before the infamous 'beachball goal' sank Rafa's men at Sunderland. Lyon inflicted more Champions League misery days later but spirits were soon restored as a brilliant Liverpool FC display sent Manchester United crashing to a 2-0 defeat. Carling Cup elimination followed at Arsenal and a nine-man LFC were then beaten in London by Roy Hodgson's Fulham.

SEASON REVIEW

NOVEMBER

A last-gasp Lyon leveller in France left Liverpool FC's Champions League dreams hanging by a thread and then two consecutive 2-2 league draws were battled out at Anfield as both Birmingham and Manchester City left with points to show for their efforts. A matchday five victory in Debrecen gave Liverpool FC the three points they needed to keep their European hopes alive - but it wasn't enough as Lyon and Fiorentina progressed from the group. Derby delight lifted spirits, however, as the Reds ran out 2-0 winners at Goodison.

DECEMBER

A disappointing month for the Reds ended with defeat in the Champions League 'dead-rubber' with Fiorentina while league defeats to Arsenal and Portsmouth did little to improve our standings in the league table. The Christmas period proved fruitful, however, with successive victories over Wolves and top-four rivals Aston Villa at Villa Park.

JANUARY

The year got off to the worst possible start as FA Cup elimination was handed out by Reading in a third round replay at Anfield. A solid string of performances over the rest of the month, however, saw three points collected from games with Tottenham and Bolton, while Wolves and Stoke proved hard to break down and each took a point from hard-fought games.

9

SEASON REVIEW

FEBRUARY

Fernando Torres netted the derby-day winner as Liverpool FC secured the league double over their Merseyside neighbours. Days later the Reds' first steps into the Europa League got underway, with a two-legged tie over Unirea safely negotiated. A tense goalless draw at Manchester City - a game in which neither side could afford to lose in the race for a top four finish - followed before Blackburn were well beaten at Anfield by a good LFC display.

MARCH

Lille were the next side to be knocked out of Europe by the Reds as a quarter-final place was comfortably secured, but the chance of competing the league double over Manchester United vanished as the Old Trafford side secured a 2-1 victory in front of their own supporters. Victory over Sunderland late in the month kept the Reds within touching distance of the sides racing for the top four places.

APRIL

Liverpool FC produced arguably their finest display of the season to brush aside the challenge of Benfica at Anfield with a second leg display of power and precision - but the dreams of a final in Hamburg were dashed by an Atletico Madrid side who broke Liverpool hearts with an extra time victory at Anfield. Successive league draws with Birmingham and Fulham did little to improve our league prospects, although the month did end on a happier note domestically as both West Ham and Burnley were soundly beaten.

MAY

The campaign ended with an Anfield defeat to Chelsea - a result which effectively handed the title to the Londoners and finished off Liverpool FC's chances of a top four finish. A final away day goalless draw at Hull rounded off the campaign.

REDS QUIZ

1 When were Liverpool FC crowned league champions for the very first time?

2 Who became the club's first player/manager?

3 'You'll Never Walk Alone' features in which famous Rogers and Hammerstein musical?

4 Milan Jovanovic has won league titles in which countries?

5 Who has made more first team appearances than any other player in the history of Liverpool FC?

6 How old was youngest-ever first team player Jack Robinson when he made his debut against Hull City in 2010?

7 Name the player who was awarded an MBE by the Queen in 2006?

8 Who was European Golden Boot winner in Season 1983/84 with 32 goals?

9 How many times has the club won the English league championship?

10 Who was the first Liverpool FC captain to lift the FA Cup?

11 What are 'Pepe' Reina's actual Christian names?

12 During his 11 years in the first team, legendary keeper Ray Clemence missed just 10 league matches. True or false?

13 Who wore the captain's armband for the victorious Community Shield clash with Chelsea in August 2006?

14 Who famously said 'I'm just one of the people on the Kop.'

15 Season 1976/77 ended victoriously with the club's first European Cup. True or false?

16 Who was the first Red since Robbie Fowler in 1996/97 to break the 30-goal barrier?

CHRISTAIN POULSEN

MARTIN SKRTEL

ROY HODGSON

How proud are you to have become only the 18th manager in our history?

I'm extremely proud. The club's tradition in terms of its football and its managers is really second to none and it was an opportunity which was absolutely impossible to turn down. I am both proud and excited at the prospect of working as the Liverpool manager.

The Fulham fans loved you but was the lure of the Liverpool FC job just too great to turn down?

I don't think there are many jobs that would have tempted me away from Fulham, to be perfectly honest. I had such a good relationship with the Chairman and the Chief Executive, the players were magnificent to work with and everything was as good as it gets, but on the other hand when there was a chance that Liverpool wanted me, and they asked to speak to me, I asked the Chairman for permission. He wasn't too happy to give it but fortunately for me this job came about and I am really happy to be here.

When did you first hear of the club's interest in you and what was your immediate thought about the possibility of one day managing Liverpool Football Club?

It was a while ago, certainly before I went to South Africa. The club has had a very diligent process. I was perhaps one of the first people they spoke to but they were determined to go through the full process and make certain that they researched everything. I'm grateful for that because it means they have chosen me having done all their homework, interviewed other candidates and plumped for me.

How did you feel when you heard of Liverpool FC's interest?

It was an enormous feeling of anticipation, expectation and then of course hope that having had the initial discussions that they would decide I was the right man for the job.

You took your first steps into management at a time when Liverpool Football Club began to dominate Europe - did you watch the likes of Bob Paisley closely and pick up anything that helped you as a manager?

What we picked up was the Liverpool style. On paper it was a relatively simple style but in actual fact simplicity is the hardest thing to achieve. Working in Sweden, as I was at the time, they were all very impressed with the quality of the passing, the quality of the movement, the way players were always available for each other. Of course the quality of the players they produced at that time, firstly Toshack and Keegan and then Dalglish and Rush, and then the great partnerships at the back with Smith, Thompson, Hansen and Lawrenson; we were brought up on that. Earlier in my career I brought a group of coaches over and Bob Paisley was great. Graeme Souness was the coach but Bob was still around at Melwood and I remember having a cup of tea with him. He was a really interesting man to meet. You can never turn the clock back and live those times again, but it would be nice if we could fashion an image again which in some way represents what these people pioneered so many years ago.

"It's a club where you feel you're not alone."

How much do you know about the traditions and history of the club and was this one of the motivating factors in your decision to come here?

It's very important you have that as a manager. At Liverpool it's highlighted really because the traditions here are so great, but even if you go to a smaller club it's still important that you're aware of what the club has done in the past and what the club means to the people. There's nowhere keener on what a club means to the people than the city of Liverpool.

You've managed the likes of Inter Milan and the Swiss and Finnish national sides - where does this job rank amongst those roles?

It'd be foolish to compare but it'd also be dishonest to say anything other than it's going to be a highlight of my career. I have worked long and hard to reach the level I have reached.

What are your main priorities on taking charge?

It's important to get started straightaway, working with the players, trying to create an environment which will give us a chance to become better and hopefully improve upon the last season.

You've been successful in many countries over Europe - what would it mean to win silverware in England with Liverpool FC?

It would mean a lot. I've never really played up my Englishness when I've been abroad. I've tried to fit in with the various cultures. I've not been one of those people saying 'We don't do it this way in England', I've always tried to avoid that, but at the same time I don't think I'll ever pretend than I'm anything other than English, so to win something in your own country would be really fantastic. If I can do it here at Liverpool it will be a real crowning glory for me.

ROY HODGSON

Did you talk to any former Liverpool FC players or staff about the job before taking it? Did Danny Murphy say anything to you before you left?

No. I was with Alan Hansen and Mark Lawrenson with the BBC but we steered well away from the subject and it was never mentioned. I've met Kenny with Christian because he was part of the process of selecting the new manager. Kenny is a person I have known for a long time, but otherwise I haven't canvassed anybody about the job simply because until Tuesday I wasn't told exactly 'We are giving you the job and everything has been agreed'. I have been very wary about speaking to people. Danny Murphy called me during this period saying he'd heard a rumour I was going to Liverpool. It was only a rumour so there was no point in talking about it.

Kenny Dalglish was key in the selection process and actually interviewed you. How much respect do you have for him and are you looking forward to working with him at Liverpool Football Club in the future?

I have a lot of respect for Kenny, as everyone has. He was arguably one of the best players ever to pull on a Liverpool shirt. He's achieved legendary status at the club and will always have a place in the hearts of Liverpool fans. It's very important for Liverpool Football Club that people like Kenny are with us, working with us and helping to promote the club and help it in every way he can. His name is up there with the true greats and deserves to be up there because he was a magnificent player.

May 1977

He enjoys instant success, leading the Swedish side to their first ever league title.

January 1982

Hodgson is appointed manager of Bristol City.

June 1985

Resigns as manager to assume the hot-seat at Malmo FF.

July 1990

Opts for a fresh challenge with Neuchatel Xamax in Switzerland.

January 1992

Hodgson is unveiled as the coach of the Swiss national team.

July 1976

28-year-old Roy Hodgson is appointed manager of Swedish club Halmstad.

May 1979

Secures a second league title before parting company with Halmstad to take up an assistant manager's role with Bristol City.

July 1983

Returns to Sweden to take charge of Orebro

May 1986

Wins the first of five consecutive league titles.

"I am both proud and excited at the prospect of working as the Liverpool manager."

The team endured a difficult season last term, losing 19 games and going out of all the cup competitions very early. What are your ambitions for this season?

The ambition initially is to do better. For Liverpool the ambition always has to be to try and achieve a Champions League place and that's what we'll be trying to do as soon as possible. There's no point in setting low goals to make yourself look a bit better if you get beyond that goal. I don't think any of the players or staff wants anything other than a successful Liverpool year and we want to hit the ground running. You can't do more than work for that. There's no point throwing out empty promises. Words are words and actions are actions and we have to show by our actions first of all on the training field and then at Anfield and other stadiums that we're ready and good enough. That's my task, to work with the players and ensure we are good enough.

Do you have a message for the Liverpool FC supporters?

The message is thank-you for having me here. I'm really looking forward to working with your team and looking forward to getting your support, which I've seen so many times throughout the years. I said recently that this is one of those clubs where your motto 'You'll Never Walk Alone' is really lived by the fans. It's a club where you feel you're not alone. I shall need lots of help and lots of support and I sincerely hope you make sure I never walk alone. That would be my message. Help me to do a good job and I'll do my best to do it.

July 1998

Leads Blackburn to a sixth-place finish and qualification for the UEFA Cup.

May 1997

Leads Inter to third place in Serie A as well as the UEFA Cup final where they are beaten on penalties by Schalke.

November 1993

Leads Switzerland to their first World Cup finals since 1966.

November 1995

Resigns from his post as Swiss national team manager.

August 1995

Guides Switzerland to Euro '96.

May 1997

Leaves his role as manager of Inter Milan.

July 1994

Treated to a hero's welcome after guiding the Swiss to the last 16 of the finals in the USA.

October 1995

It is announced that Hodgson will become the new manager of Inter Milan.

June 1997

Appointed the new manager of Blackburn Rovers.

ROY HODGSON

Martin Broughton has explained why Roy Hodgson was the number one choice to become Liverpool Football Club's 18th manager.

The Chairman lifted the lid on a rigorous interview process during which Hodgson was grilled by Christian Purslow, Kenny Dalglish and Broughton himself. In the end the board decided the former Fulham boss met every requirement outlined after Rafael Benitez's departure at the start of June. Broughton said: "You take the League Managers' Association's Manager of the Year - that shows the respect his peers have for him. It's a respect that's been earned not only over the last year, which was outstanding, but over a long period of time.

"Roy brings precisely the sort of experience we're looking for. He's been around and dealt with lots of different international players.

"He's English but he's cosmopolitan. He wasn't chosen because he was English - he was chosen because he was the best man for the job.

"We need someone to steady the ship at this stage and I think Roy has got all of the talents we were looking for."

Broughton added: "Can I just express on behalf of the club our appreciation to Mohammed Al Fayed and the Fulham team for allowing Roy to talk to us and for being so good about the whole process."

Hodgson was quickly installed as the bookies' favourite once the Anfield hotseat became vacant - but Broughton revealed the board started their search with an open mind. He said: "We didn't start off with a first choice. We wanted to have a proper and professional process. We didn't say A was favourite or B was favourite. We talked to quite a lot of people.

December 1998

Sacked as manager of Blackburn Rovers with the club rooted to the foot of the Premier League table.

May 1999

Comes to Inter Milan's aid as caretaker manager in the final month of the 98-99 season.

July 1999

Joins Swiss side Grasshopper as manager

July 2000

Moves to Denmark to take over at Copenhagen.

May 2001

Leads Copenhagen to the Danish Superliga championship.

June 2001

Returns to Italy to take the helm at Udinese.

December 2001

Dismissed as manager after less than six months in the job.

April 2002

Named as coach of the United Arab Emirates.

January 2004

Sacked following a disappointing Gulf Cup campaign.

May 2004

Named as manager of Norwegian outfit, Viking.

"Roy brings precisely the sort of experience we're looking for."

"There were a lot of applicants and we approached some others. There were a number of telephone interviews to get a shortlist. Then there were a number of face-to-face interviews which Christian Purslow and Kenny Dalglish carried out.

"They put their conclusions to the board and the board agreed it would be a good idea for me and Christian to meet the last two. Roy was our choice."

One man who wanted the job was Kenny Dalglish. Asked if the man known as King would now stay in his ambassadorial role through the Hodgson era, Broughton responded: "Yes. Kenny put his name in for it. He wanted the job. We appreciate the fact he wanted to do it but for us he was never a candidate. I explained that to him.

"Kenny has an excellent future at this club. He's happy in his current ambassadorial role and we would like to build on that role. We haven't defined what that building will be because that's for Roy and Kenny. They know each other from a long time back."

August 2005
Agrees a deal to take charge of the Finnish national team.

December 2007
Appointed manager of Fulham.

November 2007
Refuses the chance to remain as Finland coach after failing to qualify for Euro 2008.

May 2008
Leads Fulham to safety after a Danny Murphy header gives them a 1-0 win at Portsmouth.

May 2009
Guides Fulham to seventh place - their highest ever Premier League finish. The club also qualify for the Europa League.

March 2010
Leads Fulham into the Europa League quarter-finals with a sensational 4-1 second-leg success over Italian giants Juventus.

May 2010
Hodgson is named the LMA Manager of the Year for 2009-10.

July 2010
Appointed manager of Liverpool Football Club.

FERNANDO TORRES

"...everyone knows I am really happy here and really happy to play at Anfield."

Congratulations on winning the World Cup - did you have a good summer?

Yes, as you can imagine it was an amazing day for Spaniards all over the world. Winning the World Cup happens maybe once in your life so it was a fantastic feeling and a great way to end the season. I have had a break over the summer and I'm now glad to be back here at Liverpool FC to see all of my teammates.

We obviously have a new manager now who you met in Spain. How impressed are you with Roy Hodgson's plans for the club and how much are you looking forward to working with him?

I really appreciated the fact that Roy came out to see me while I was on my holidays. He told me about his plans for the club and what he wanted from me and I appreciated that. I hope he will be the right man to reach the targets of Liverpool FC and I am really looking forward to working with him.

Steven Gerrard has already said he is excited about the season, Joe Cole has arrived - how excited are you about the future here at Liverpool Football Club?

I think Joe is exactly the kind of player we need to improve the history of our club. We are keeping our best players and so it's nice to be back with them. Hopefully we can play together regularly.

"This is the best club in the country so the targets and expectations are always high."

How excited were you when you heard Joe Cole was signing for Liverpool FC?

He is the kind of player I like to play with and the kind of player who can take the team to a higher level. His passing is unbelievable so hopefully he can start the season well because I am sure he will be a key player for us.

Joe has said he's looking forward to creating a lot of chances and a lot of goals for you this season...

Hopefully that will be the case. I'm excited about playing with him and hopefully we can all help him settle into the team and the city to make sure he can reach his best as quickly as possible. It's up to us to help the new players.

What are your personal targets this season and what do you think Liverpool FC can achieve?

This is the best club in the country so the targets and expectations are always high. Hopefully we can stay at our level. At Liverpool Football Club the aim is to fight for every title. It was difficult last season but we are sure we can improve this season. I am really happy to be back, really happy to stay with all my teammates. My commitment and loyalty to the club and to the fans is the same as it was on my first day when I signed. I am looking forward to the challenge ahead.

Why does this club mean so much to you?

From my first day I got the same welcome as Stevie or Carra or players who have been here for a long time. I felt at home from the first day, I feel the fans love me and everyone knows I am really happy here and really happy to play at Anfield. As I said earlier, I'm looking forward to playing with my teammates and for the fans.

Is the dream to score the goals which wins trophies for this club?

Of course. I know that one trophy here at Liverpool FC - maybe the Premier League - means more than three or four with another club. This was my target from the day I came and it's still my target. Hopefully this season we can feel this sensation here at Liverpool Football Club.

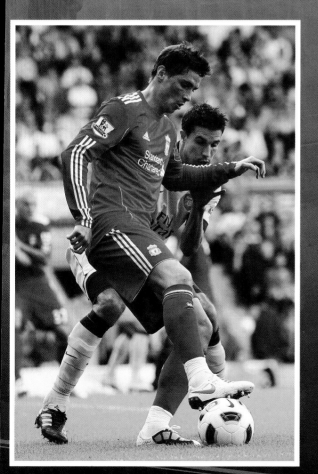

LUCAS LEIVA

Lucas Leiva has set himself the target of contributing more goals as he looks forward to the 2010-11 season.

••••••••••••••••••••••••••••••••••••

The Brazilian midfielder - who was crowned LFC Young Player of the Season last term - managed only one goal during the campaign, albeit a brilliant effort in the 4-1 win against Benfica at Anfield. His goals tally is something he's looking to improve.

"It was a good goal against Benfica," he recalled. "To be honest though, I have been a bit unlucky with the goals. I could have scored more than I have. I have had a few chances, but unfortunately couldn't score.

"At least I have been in some scoring positions so hopefully next season if I have these kind of opportunities, I will take more and be able to contribute more goals in the season."

Disappointing goalscoring statistics aside, Lucas has blossomed into a key first team player at Anfield over recent months and he admits he's relishing the challenge of improving further and silencing those who question his position in the team.

"I've learned a lot more about myself and become a stronger person and player. It has made me desperate to prove people wrong," he said.

"There have been times (in the past) when I thought I may have made the wrong decision but now I am sure that I have made the right one.

"My game has changed a lot since leaving Brazil. I was able to attack more at Gremio because I played with two defensive midfielders, In England you have more responsibility.

"I've learned a lot more about myself and become a stronger person and player."

"I still think I have some work to do if all the fans are going to believe in me. I'm happy and I feel I'm improving. But it isn't about me, it's about the club doing well."

Former midfielder Sammy Lee, however, insists the decision of the fans to crown Lucas as their young star of last season was justified.

"It's nice to see him getting some reward," he said. "Our fans appreciate what the boy has done.

"He doesn't get the accolades he deserves from enough people within the game, but certainly our supporters know.

"They've seen the progress he's made, the determination, commitment and work rate in each and every game, and I think he's come on in leaps and bounds this season.

"I think he's improved most on the ball - he's got great skill on the ball. He's affecting the play more now with switching of play and penetrating passes. I think overall his possession and use of the ball has been superb."

JOE COLE

How pleased are you to be a Liverpool FC player?

Very pleased. I set myself a deadline to make a decision and when I made it I sent a text to Christian Purslow and Steven Gerrard and then turned my phone off. I know I have made the right decision and I am looking forward to the challenge. This is a challenge for me. I have played in London all my life, I could have stayed at Chelsea because the fans loved me and I won things, but I wanted to challenge myself and when I knew Liverpool were interested it was a no-brainer because they are the biggest club in the country.

This is a massive club. I tried to take everything out of the equation, take the financial and location side out and just thought in football terms. I thought about the semi-final of the Champions League in 2005 when I ran onto the field and the hairs on the back of my neck stood up. I was thinking about playing in that atmosphere every week and that swung it for me.

How will you feel to have the fans who made so much noise in that semi-final on your side now?

That's the thing I am looking forward to. You talk to Liverpool players and talk about the European nights. I experienced it as an opponent and it was immense. To go out there and play in that atmosphere every week will be phenomenal.

Did Roy Hodgson have to sell the club to you - or does the club sell itself?

I had a chat with the gaffer about football and was impressed with him. The club has had Spanish and French managers over the years and I think it's a breath of fresh air to get an Englishman in. The club finished seventh last year which wasn't good enough and he explained where the club wanted to go. I jumped on board because with the players we have here and the players we are looking to bring in, it's definitely going in the right direction.

With the amount of experience Roy has as a manager, how do you think he can help you move on to another level?

We have talked about positions in the team and types of formations he wants to play and I just want to be part of the team. I want to go out there and to run and fight for the lads and the fans. That's what I'll always do and Roy is the man who can make sure we are a nice unit as a team. It's all about us and being together as a team and having the spirit which can take you a long way. If you add that to the quality players we've got here we can go a long way.

> *"I think players can play for other clubs but with Liverpool you have to live and breathe it. It's that kind of a place."*

Does it excite you when you look through the names in the LFC squad?

Yes, definitely. I am used to playing with world class players. I am excited about playing with Fernando and obviously I know Stevie, Carra and Jonno from the England set-up. Pepe Reina, Aquilani, there are a lot of big name players here but I will need time to settle down and relax into the club. I can guarantee the fans I will be giving 100 per cent every game. I am proud to be playing for this club and will give my all in every training session and every game to help the club be successful and put some pots in the trophy cabinet.

JOE COLE

"He's one of the best attacking midfield players in England"

The day after you signed Steven Gerrard committed his future to Liverpool FC - how much did that mean to you?

That was the best bit of news I could have had. I know Stevie, he is Liverpool through and through and I know from playing with him and against him for the last ten years what a quality player he is. I know how much this club means to him. I think players can play for other clubs but with Liverpool you have to live and breathe it. It's that kind of a place. I am excited by the challenge. I am moving my family and everyone is excited and booking their weekends up here. I am going to make it work

How big a move is it for you to move up north?

It's a massive deal. We've just had a young baby girl, but I'm 28 now and I have a good family around me. I know people will make me feel welcome and the response I have had has been amazing. I just want to get involved. When you move to a new club it's important to immerse yourself into everything about it and that's what I'll be looking to do. I know the fans are great with the players and I will fight to try and win trophies for this club.

"I'm proud to wear the number ten shirt. I'd have been proud to wear any Liverpool shirt, to be honest."

You have been given the number 10 shirt - what does that mean to you?

I'm proud to wear the number ten shirt. I'd have been proud to wear any Liverpool shirt, to be honest. When I was growing up we were just coming out of the era when Liverpool were winning titles on a regular basis, but I know all about it and I'll be proud to wear the shirt. It'll be strange to pull on the red shirt for a change but I'm looking forward to it and looking forward to being given time to settle in. I just want to help the team to do things.

JOE COLE

What do you think you can bring to the team and how much can you improve here?

I'd like to make a lot of chances for Fernando and the front boys. I don't want to say I'll do this and that, I'll just say the fans will have a player who is going to give his all. From what I hear, that's all the people want. I want to be a success here and I'll do everything I can for the team to make it work.

Do you think you are entering the peak stages of your career?

Yes, definitely. I've had a tough two seasons with injury and one of the factors in my decision was coming to a club where I'd be able to string 90 minutes together. Your body needs to get used to the sharpness of doing it week in week out. I've had a difficult couple of years but I'm coming here as an experienced player who is still fresh and excited about it.

Do you set yourself targets?

I do but I'll keep them to myself. In football you can have a bad game or a great game, but for myself I want to be part of a team that's going to win things. It's important this team is challenging and that we're right there at the end. That's my target - to play as many games as I can in this team and achieve something great.

Have you always enjoyed the banter with the fans at Anfield?

You do get some stick. Over the last couple of years I've been warming up a lot down the touchline and the stick does make me chuckle. I love it and hopefully they will be saying nice things about me now.

What's your message to Liverpool FC fans?

I know what they want and know they want a team to be proud of. I'll go out there every day and live and breathe the club and give my all. I just want to get myself fit, I'm a bit behind in my training work but I want to get fit and help the team to achieve something. I want to be part of a team that's capable of doing great things.

"I am proud to be playing for this club and will give my all"

Roy Hodgson on Joe Cole

Roy Hodgson has revealed how the lure of Liverpool Football Club was the key factor in enticing one of the 'best midfielders in the country.'

The Reds boss could not hide his delight after securing the signature of Joe Cole on a free transfer and was quick to point out that the former Chelsea star's wages were not the main motivation behind his move to Anfield.

"I'm very pleased because any concern that it was going to turn into an auction all about money quickly disappeared after myself and Christian Purslow had a long conversation with Joe," Hodgson said.

"Obviously he is going to be a high wage earner because he is a free transfer - he was at his previous club - and he would be worth a lot of money on the transfer market.

"We wanted to make it clear that we wanted him for football reasons and only if he fitted in with our wage structure.

"I'm pleased to say that Joe has chosen Liverpool to come and play football - and not because of the money. That's a very satisfying thing for me as a manager and for the club itself."

Cole's arrival is expected to add a new dimension to the Reds attack and Hodgson is relishing the prospect of working with a player he regards as one of the Barclays Premier League's finest stars. "He's one of the best attacking midfield players in England," he said.

"His appearances for Chelsea and England over the years have shown that. He's a player that can play in a number of attacking positions, which is very useful.

"He's a quality player. People will talk about qualities in different ways, but for me he has an all round quality that makes him a good player and one we hope we can get a lot of use out of this year."

GLEN JOHNSON

SPOT THE BALL

Can you use your skills to spot the correct ball in the image below?

The Answers page 61

AT THE WORLD CUP

The 2010 World Cup may well have climaxed with Fernando Torres and Pepe Reina being crowned champions - but what were the other key contributions made by Liverpool FC players in South Africa?

To celebrate the feast of football that was on show at Africa's first ever tournament, we've put together a short compilation of what we feel were the highlights for those who usually ply their trade on Merseyside.

GERRARD V USA

It all started so well for England didn't it?
With just four minutes on the clock of their first group match against the USA, Steven Gerrard got Fabio Capello's men off to a flyer when he stabbed home the opener following a typical forward burst from central midfield.

However, an error from goalkeeper Robert Green would deny Stevie the joy of being England's matchwinner and there would be few highlights from there on in, as the Three Lions bowed out with a crushing defeat to Germany in the last 16.

DIRK DOWNS AGGER'S DANES

In a match that saw Dirk Kuyt go head-to-head with club-mate Daniel Agger, it was the flying Dutchman who came out on top.

The striker turned wideman sealed a 2-0 victory with a close range finish after Agger had inadvertently deflected Simon Poulsen's poor defensive header into his own net to give Holland the lead within seconds of the restart.

SKRTEL'S BLOCK

Martin Skrtel's Slovakia produced one of the upsets of the tournament as they booked their place in the knockout stage at the expense of holders Italy at Ellis Park. The Reds defender played a vital role in his country's 3-2 victory, completing a sensational goal-line clearance to deny the Azzurri with Slovakia just the one goal ahead.

JOVA STUNS GERMANY

Milan Jovanovic gave LFC fans a taste of what is hopefully set to come, when he fired home a close range volley to give Serbia a shock 1-0 win over 10-man Germany in the group stage. The man nicknamed 'le serpent' slammed home a 35th minute effort after Nikola Zigic had nodded Milan Krasic's fine cross into his path. However, it would prove to be the only highlight for our new No. 14 as the Serbs bowed out of the competition after losing their final group match with Australia.

DIRK ASSIST SENDS SKRTEL HOME

Dirk Kuyt notched an assist as Holland booked a quarter-final place at the expense of Skrtel's Slovakia. The unsung hero of Oranje broke clear six minutes from time and unselfishly laid the ball into the path of Wesley Sneijder to coolly slot into an empty net. It put the Dutch two goals to the good and proved to be the defining moment of the match as Slovakia grabbed a consolation deep into injury-time.

DIRK DOES IT AGAIN

Having already made a huge impact on Holland's march to the last eight, Kuyt further endeared himself to his country's army of supporters when he once again came up with the crucial assist to see off much-fancied Brazil.

The Reds No.18 provided the flick on from Arjen Robben's corner for Sneijder to nod home the winner after the Inter Milan man had cancelled out Robinho's superb first-half opener.

KUYT FLYING HIGH AS DUTCH BOOK FINAL BERTH

Kuyt completed a remarkable hat-trick of key assists when he provided the cross for Robben to nod home Holland's third goal in their 3-2 semi-final win over Uruguay.

It meant the 29-year-old had laid on the winning goal in all three of his country's knockout matches en route to the final, a contribution that saw him finish joint top of the assists leaderboard.

SPANISH DUO REJOICE

Fernando Torres played the final 15 minutes of extra-time as a substitute as Spain beat Holland 1-0 to secure the 2010 World Cup.

The Reds striker endured a bittersweet moment as the ecstasy of playing a small part in Andres Iniesta's winner was juxtaposed by the frustration of pulling up with an adductor injury just seconds before the full-time whistle.

Liverpool stopper Pepe Reina - who remained an unused substitute throughout the tournament - was heavily involved in the celebrations, while Dirk Kuyt and Ryan Babel could only look on in despair.

DAVID NGOG

Liverpool FC striker David Ngog admits he is enjoying the challenge of trying to establish himself as a Premier League striker

. . . .

The French youngster was a regular member of the squad last season when he deputised for the injured Fernando Torres, but rather than feeling burdened by the challenge he admits he embraced the opportunity to impress in the Reds' forward-line.

"I enjoy the challenge because this is what I want, to play and score goals for Liverpool," Ngog said.

"I want to take the responsibility and show what I can do for the team.

"Liverpool is one of the best teams in Europe so to score goals for them makes me happy."

"It gives me a really good feeling when I score goals for Liverpool and I want to get many more. It's great to be able to share it with my teammates and the supporters.

"Liverpool is one of the best teams in Europe so to score goals for them makes me happy."

Ngog has now clocked up more than 50 games for LFC and is hoping to make an even bigger impact on the first team over the coming months.

"No game in the Premier League is ever simple, but especially away from home," he added.

"A lot of the teams are very physical and make you fight for everything.

"You have to be strong and really battle to get possession and keep it until your teammates can get forward in support. It wasn't something I found easy at first.

"Now I think I am getting stronger in those situations. The more experience you have of playing like that the more confident you become."

He added: "I think I'm becoming a better player and know I need to do that. If I can I will be happy.

DAVID NGOG

"I've managed to score some goals which is pleasing. But that's what people expect of strikers, it's our job. Hopefully I can get more in the future."

Ngog's early displays in a Red shirt - which have included a goal against Manchester United at Anfield - have already drawn admiration from Ian Rush, the Anfield scoring legend.
"The most obvious quality is that he can score goals," said Rush, who scored 346 times in 660 games for Liverpool.
"David is still rough around the edges, but the Anfield coaching staff are clearly working hard on him and he has undoubted potential.

"The experience of scoring a winning goal against United will only help his development."

"It gives me a really good feeling when I score goals for Liverpool and I want to get many more. It's great to be able to share it with my teammates and the supporters.

MILAN JOVANOVIC

Serbian striker Milan Jovanovic has insisted the departure of Rafael Benitez never made him doubt his decision to sign for Liverpool Football Club

It was the former Reds' boss who secured Jovanovic's signing on a free transfer from Standard Liege during the summer, but even when Benitez left Anfield Jovanovic knew exactly where he wanted his footballing future to lie.

"I chose to sign for Liverpool Football Club, and that is it. It's very simple," he said

"Liverpool was always my biggest wish and to be here is a great day in my career and in my life. I knew they were following my games for Standard Liege and also the Belgium national side and when they first made contact with me I was very happy. Liverpool was my only choice and I'm pleased the negotiations were successful. Now I want to do as well as I can for the club over the next three years.

"When you speak about Liverpool you are speaking about one of the biggest clubs in the world - maybe for me, the biggest. You are talking about an historical club which has won the Champions League five times.

"I can't wait to play at Anfield and hear 'You'll Never Walk Alone' - the best song in the world.

"I also can't wait to play with players like Torres, Gerrard, Kuyt, Mascherano and Reina - some of the best players in the world.

"It's hard for me to tell the fans what I can bring to the team, I'd prefer to leave that talking to someone else. But I know I need to be good on the pitch and show my quality when I get the chance.

"I'm looking forward to working with the new manager, with all the players and hopefully being successful together and winning trophies."

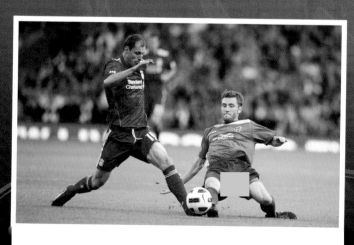

> *"I can't wait to play at Anfield and hear 'You'll Never Walk Alone' - the best song in the world."*

Hodgson on Jovanovic

Roy Hodgson has revealed his delight at Milan Jovanovic's Anfield arrival - and admitted he was tracking the Serbian striker while manager at Fulham.

"I'm very pleased we have got Milan," said Hodgson. "He looks a very keen and enthusiastic player and it's good to have players who are desperate to play for the club.

"I was not responsible for signing him but I was pleased to hear the club had taken the initiative to get a player like him. I've seen him a lot during my time at Fulham and we were watching him.

"He's a natural wide player who can play through the middle. He's more of an attacking winger than a wide midfielder and he's a goalscorer. He scores goals for club and country and I'm sure we'll get a lot of use out of him.
"He scored in the World Cup, he's done well with Standard Liege at Champions League level, so he's no stranger to the big games."

> *"When you speak about Liverpool you are speaking about one of the biggest clubs in the world - maybe for me, the biggest."*

STEVEN GERRARD

SPOT THE DIFFERENCE

Can you spot the seven differences below?

The Answers page 61

MAXI RODRIGUEZ

Maxi Rodriguez has revealed how he believes the aggressive nature of the Barclays Premier League will bring out the best in him.

The Argentina winger has made a positive impression at Anfield since signing at the start of the year from Atletico Madrid.

And rather than be put off by the notoriously physical style of English football, Maxi admits it's something he is relishing.

"It's going fantastic so far and I couldn't have hoped for better," he said. "It's so different to daily life in Madrid, but I think I am settling in and it's even better here than I expected it to be.

"Gradually as the weeks have gone by, I've been getting used to daily life in the city. I think it will be even better when I'm more settled.

"It's totally different here to the football in La Liga. Certainly you are aware of the fact it is a lot more physical, tougher and aggressive - they are the big differences.

"But wherever you play football in the world, you still play with a round ball, so you get used to it.

"What's more, I really like the competitive, physical aspect of the game. I think it suits my style and I'm enjoying it."

Liverpool fans have also enjoyed Maxi's early days in a Liverpool shirt - and he admits he has loved the buzz of playing at Anfield.

"All home games are special occasions for the players and fans, but you play with your heart on those occasions because you know how much it means to the supporters," he added.

"It's something special to hear the fans singing You'll Never Walk Alone.

"I'd been here with Atletico in the Champions League, but obviously I was on the opposition. You really appreciate this tradition when you know the fans are on your side and singing on your behalf.

"It's a beautiful moment and a special experience for both fans and players. It's a real motivating factor and something that should continue for all of Liverpool's existence. It's unique and special."

"It's something special to hear the fans singing You'll Never Walk Alone."

Maxi was greeted by a few familiar faces at Melwood when he completed his move to Anfield · most notably international colleague Javier Mascherano.

"When you come to a different club in a different country and you don't understand the language, it's a big help to have someone around who can translate for you," he added.

"However, the big thing is to try on your own, and so when I am out and about I try to learn. I also have a teacher and I'm having lessons, and bit by bit I'll get used to speaking.

"Speaking is hard so far, but my understanding is coming along." Meanwhile, the forward has revealed the reasoning behind the decision to display 'Maxi' on the back of his jersey rather than 'Rodriguez'.

"I am fine with Maxi, but fans can call me whatever they prefer," he said. "We tend to have lots of nicknames in Argentina. Mine is 'La Fiera', while Javier's is 'the boss' or 'El Jefe'. It's a tradition over there for players to have a nickname."

JONJO SHELVEY

Jonjo Shelvey has spoken of his determination to make an instant impact at Anfield as he prepares for his first season in the top flight of English football.

The 18-year-old England youth international signed for the Reds at the back end of last season and is now looking forward to his first taste of life as a Premier League player.

Regarded by many as one of the brightest young talents in English football - and described by his former Academy Manager as a player in the Steven Gerrard mould - the attacking midfielder arrived on Merseyside with a blossoming reputation, and he insists he won't be wasting any time in attempting to prove his worth at Anfield.

Shelvey said: "Being at Liverpool is what every kid dreams of. When I was in school and in the playground I used to pretend to be players like Steven Gerrard, so it's unreal to think I'll be training with these players day in and day out.

"At Charlton training was just shooting and 5-a-sides and I was getting home at 1pm. At Liverpool we're not getting home till 2pm or 3pm and that's what I needed. I needed to be somewhere where I could learn about the game because it got to the point where I wasn't learning at Charlton. I'm glad to be around the best people you could possibly be around.

"I'm really excited and can't wait for the season to start now."

"Being at Liverpool is what every kid dreams of."

"I'm really excited and can't wait for the season to start now. I want to get at least 20 games under my belt this season so I can start getting myself into it. I am confident, you have to be. When you are 18-years of age and you are getting thrown into games at Anfield then you can't have any fear. You have to go and do what you do."

Having represented England at both U16 and U17 levels, Shelvey became Charlton's youngest ever player before going on to net eight goals in 49 appearances for the London club.

A softly-spoken but fiercely determined youngster, Shelvey is clearly confident of succeeding on the pitch at Anfield - but how has he coped with crossing the north-south divide?

"Obviously it's a different lifestyle compared to being at Charlton," he said. "The training is harder, everyone is a top quality professional, so it's totally different. It's different but I'm enjoying it. It's hard but I'm coping with it and it's good to be here.

JONJO SHELVEY

"I thought I would find it a lot harder but I've had a lot of help from the club. I have my mum and dad coming up which makes it a lot easier. My dad comes up on a Monday and Tuesday and then I'll take him to Lime Street station on a Wednesday morning before training. My mum then comes up and she'll be there when I get home, which is great because she loves to cook.

"It still hasn't really sunk in now that I could be playing in the Premier League week in and week out. It's unreal."

He may now be dreaming of pulling on the red shirt, but it was only four years ago when the self-confessed West Ham fan was left distraught at the hands of Liverpool as Steven Gerrard snatched FA Cup glory away from the Hammers with a last-gasp equaliser in Cardiff.

"I was away in Italy with Charlton at the time of that game and we watched it in a pub. There were a few Liverpool fans in there and they were rubbing it in all day," he recalls.

"I may be a West Ham fan but when you watch Liverpool on the television and hear the crowd singing it gives you goose-pimples. It will be amazing to play there. I can't wait. I'll probably faint before I walk out."

And when Shelvey does realise his dream and make his debut in a Liverpool FC shirt, what can the fans expect?

"I'm glad to be around the best people you could possibly be around."

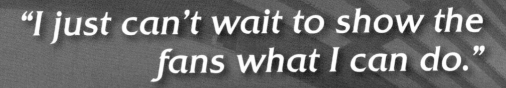

"I just can't wait to show the fans what I can do."

"I'm an all-action player," he says. "I can defend, although I'd rather be bombing on to score goals and create things. I used to play in the hole behind the striker at Charlton but I prefer to play in central midfield to dictate the play.

"From watching the Premier League on the television you seem to get a lot more time and space on the ball compared to League One and that will suit me."

"I just can't wait to show the fans what I can do."

MARTIN KELLY

Martin Kelly admits the arrival of Roy Hodgson has given Liverpool FC's young stars a lift as they try to prove their worth to the new manager.

Kelly was given an early chance to impress his new boss when he was named in the squad which went through their pre-season paces in Switzerland - and he admits he is relishing the chance to stake a claim for regular first-team action in 2010/11.

He said: "It's an exciting time. It's always exciting for a young player at this time of the season because a new manager has come in and it starts with a clean slate.

"He seems a great manager. He's easy to understand and some of his coaching points have helped us all.

"He knows so much about the game and it's great, especially for us young players, to learn off a manager with such experience. It can only be good for us.

"This is our chance to show what we can do and when you get a chance, you've got to take it."

After making three first-team appearances last season, including a highly-impressive Champions League run out against Lyon at Anfield, Kelly is eager for more senior action this term. He added: "I'd like to be in the first-team squad regularly, in the Premier League and European games, and hopefully get more than a few games under my belt.

"If there are injuries, I hope the manager can look to me and throw me in without expecting me to flop. He can rely on me now if need be."

"This is our chance to show what we can do"

CROSSWORD

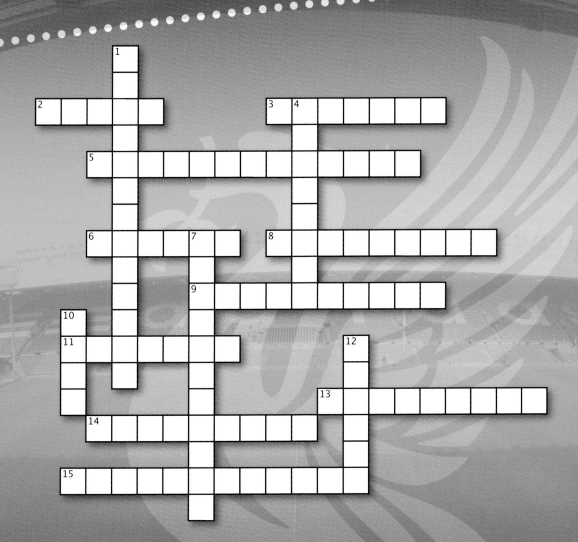

Across

2. Vice-captain's first name
3. Joe Cole was club captain here
5. Club legend signed from Celtic
6. Daniel Agger played here in Denmark
8. Dirk Kuyt's former Dutch club
9. Scottish birthplace of Danny Wilson
11. Liverpool FC record goal scorer
13. Player born in Madrid
14. Scorer against Germany in South African World Cup
15. Most first team appearances

Down

1. Glen Johnson debuted at this ground
4. Number of times League Champions
7. Legendary manager
10. Number of times European Champions
12. Number of goals scored in record victory

The Answers page 61

DR BRUKNER

While Roy Hodgson and his staff are working all the hours to ensure the players perform on the field, off it a new team has been put together to help ensure the manager can call on his stars more often than ever before.

●●●●●●●●●●●●●●●●●●●●●●●●●●●●●●●●●

With many players falling foul of injuries over recent seasons, a new focus has been placed on the need to keep the Reds' squad fit and fresh as they look to embark on a quest for glory at home and abroad.

Dr Peter Brukner, the new Head of Sports Medicine and Sports Science at Anfield, has brought ten new members of staff with him to completely revamp Liverpool FC's medical set-up - and the highly respected Australian doctor admits he is relishing the challenge which lies ahead on Merseyside.

"It's not something I had planned and it came completely out of the blue," said Brukner, who was appointed in March. "I was contacted by Liverpool and initially I said come back in 18 months time.

"I've got four kids (Julia, Charlie, Joe and Bill) and my youngest still has 18 months left in school. My wife, Diana, and I vaguely thought about coming over here after that but never did anything specific about it as we had a very good life in Australia.

"But Liverpool were persistent and I guess what attracted me was the challenge, the opportunity to oversee the full medical outfit rather than just being the team doctor. I've always felt that the English Premier League was just a little bit behind in its approach.

"By that I mean injury management and injury prevention. It's something I had picked up from the guys at the Socceroos; the reason they always enjoyed coming back was because they knew they were going to get some good treatment.

"I always felt that I would love to get my hands on a Premier League club and I thought I would be able to make a difference. If I didn't think I could make a difference, I wouldn't be here. It's all about the challenge.

"The other thing was the faith that the club had in me. I think it was quite a radical step to get someone in to completely overhaul the department.

"They had put a lot more financial resources into the sports medicine and sports science department.

"They have supported me in increasing the staff and improving the equipment. They were very supportive so, with that, I thought I've got the challenge, let's have a crack at it."

"I always felt that I would love to get my hands on a Premier League club and I thought I would be able to make a difference."

DR BRUKNER

Having founded the biggest sports medicine clinic of its kind, co-written a book on sports medicine, penned a weekly column about injuries in Australian Rules Football for The Melbourne Age newspaper, and acted as radio pundit in his homeland, Dr Brukner clearly arrives at Anfield with a glowing reputation.

And he is well aware his job is to keep the players fit, fresh and ready to play whenever the manager wants to call upon them.

"There are two aspects to it," he added. "We will be judged by the success of the team as well. But specifically our performance indicators are the number of what we regard as preventable injuries, soft tissue ones like hamstrings and groins.

"If someone comes along, kicks a player in the shin and breaks their leg, there's nothing we can do about that! But we believe that with proper conditioning we can reduce the number of muscle injuries and other such problems.

"Maybe it is going to take a year or two to get everything in place that we really want to but ultimately that is the aim. Everything has been great so far and everyone has been incredibly welcoming. We have changed a lot of things and people have been very accepting of that change.

"I've brought a lot of new staff in like the head of fitness Darren Burgess, who was with me at the Socceroos, and head physiotherapist Phil Coles. A lot of people had left with Rafa so that gave us an opportunity to bring in some high quality staff.

"We've got a fantastic group of people here and one of the big qualities is that they all work well together. The medical and fitness department have got to be a team within a team – all you need is one person who is doing it for other reasons and it can go wrong.

"We've all got to communicate really well, so we meet every morning and then I will go and tell the manager what is going on. It's going to be good."

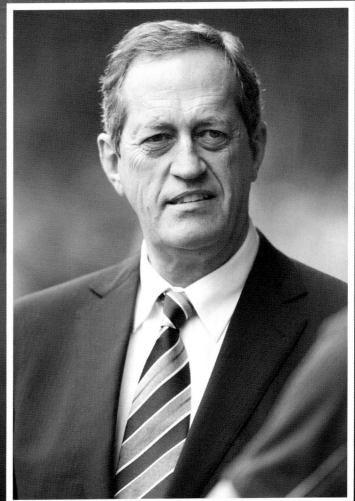

"We've got a fantastic group of people here and one of the big qualities is that they all work well together."

JAMIE CARRAGHER

THE ANSWERS

REDS QUIZ pg 12

1. 1901
2. Kenny Dalglish
3. Carousel
4. Russia and Belgium
5. Ian Callaghan – with an astonishing 857
6. 16 years, 250 days old
7. Steven Gerrard
8. Ian Rush
9. 18 times
10. Ron Yeats
11. Jose Manuel
12. False – it was only 6
13. Jamie Carragher
14. Bill Shankly
15. True
16. Fernando Torres

SPOT THE BALL pg 33

SPOT THE DIFFERENCE pg 47

CROSSWORD pg 55

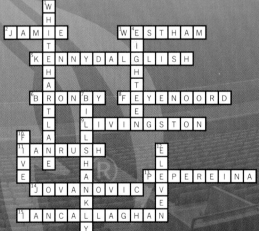

YOU'LL NEVER WALK ALONE

LIVERPOOL FOOTBALL CLUB

EST·1892